D1721076

Mit Wörterbuch und Vokabelhilfe

Elisabeth Zöller

Abenteuergeschichten

Aus dem Deutschen übersetzt von David Ingram

Zeichnungen von Wilfried Gebhard

Bibliografische Information Der Deutschen Bibliothek
Die Deutsche Bibliothek verzeichnet diese Publikation in der Deutschen Nationalbibliografie; detaillierte bibliografische Daten sind im Internet über *http://dnb.ddb.de* abrufbar.

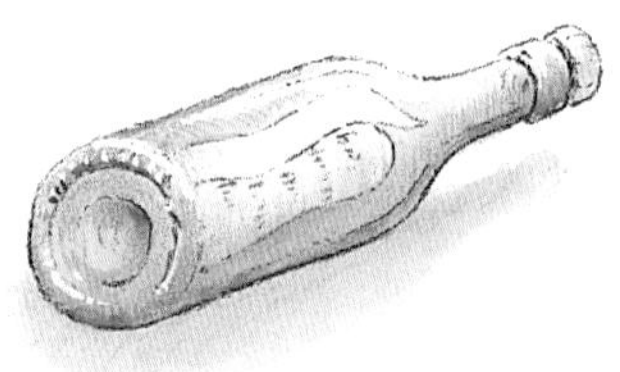

Der Umwelt zuliebe ist dieses Buch auf chlorfrei gebleichtem Papier gedruckt.

ISBN 3-7855-5333-1 – 1. Auflage 2005

Die deutsche Originalausgabe erschien 1999 im Loewe Verlag unter dem Titel „Leselöwen-Abenteuergeschichten"
Aus dem Deutschen übersetzt von David Ingram
Umschlagillustration: Wilfried Gebhard
Umschlaggestaltung: Andreas Henze

www.loewe-verlag.de

Contents

Liebe Eltern,

unaufhaltsam hält die englische Sprache Einzug in den kindlichen Wortschatz. Was die Sprachwissenschaft nüchtern als Anglizismen betitelt, finden die Kinder überaus spannend. Mit ungebremstem Wissensdurst machen sie sich daran, erste Worte oder Sätze in einer Fremdsprache zu erlernen und zu kommunizieren.

Kinder sind relativ früh mit dem Englischen vertraut, spätestens seit der Einführung des Englischunterrichts an den Grundschulen. Eine Fremdsprache spielerisch, ohne Erfolgszwang, dafür aber mit schnellen Erfolgserlebnissen lernen, so lautet das Motto.
Dieses Prinzip haben wir auch den Englisch-Ausgaben unserer Erstlese-Reihe *Leselöwen* zu Grunde gelegt. In abgeschlossenen Geschichten können die kindlichen Leser ihre ersten Englischkenntnisse anwenden und vertiefen. Die Sprache ist einfach gehalten, die wichtigsten Vokabeln sind im Text markiert und werden in ihrer konkreten Bedeutung am Rand auf Deutsch erklärt. Verben werden dabei gleich in der jeweiligen Person, Adjektive in der flektierten

Form übersetzt. Der Sinn eines Satzes lässt sich so schnell und ohne lästiges Nachschlagen erschließen. Viele Begriffe werden zusätzlich in den Illustrationen durch Wort-Bildzuweisungen erläutert.
Im Anhang finden sich sowohl die wichtigsten Vokabeln aus dem Text in alphabetischer Reihenfolge als auch ein speziell dem jeweiligen Thema zu Grunde gelegter Wortschatz auf einer praktischen Ausklappseite.
Die Verben stehen hier im Infinitiv, da an dieser Stelle der Hauptakzent eher auf der Erweiterung des Wortschatzes als auf der Erschließung eines Wortes innerhalb eines Satzes liegt. Dabei werden nicht alle möglichen Bedeutungen im Deutschen angegeben, sondern nur die wichtigsten.
Und wenn Sie mit Ihrem Kind gleichzeitig auch das Hörverständnis und die Sprechfertigkeit trainieren möchten, sind bei Jumbo zu jedem englischen *Leselöwen*-Band die entsprechenden Hörkassetten erhältlich.

Viel Spaß und Erfolg mit
„Englisch lernen mit den Leselöwen"
wünscht Ihnen Ihr

Leselöwen-Englisch-Team

flame

Fire alarm

Stefan is out in the street very late at night. It's ten o'clock! He missed his train, and then his bus. There are not very many trains or buses on Sundays.

verpasste

Now Stefan has to walk home alone through the village. He telephones his Granny and tells her that he is late. She says to him: "Walk back through the village. See you later."

Großmutter

zu spät kommt

Stefan has to wait nearly one hour for the bus. It finally arrives.

endlich

Stefan is glad that his Granny isn't worried about him. Not like his mother. She always makes a fuss about things. Stefan doesn't like that.

Großmutter
sich keine Sorgen um ihn macht
wie
macht viel Aufhebens um

The bus stops in the village. Stefan knows the way to his Granny's house. He crosses the marketplace.

überquert

There's a funny smell in the air. Maybe someone is having a barbecue somewhere.

Grillparty

"Go to your Granny's house," Stefan says to himself.

But there's such a strong smell in the air. It smells like a fire! Stefan looks round. There's no one about, and the marketplace is empty and dark.

Es ist niemand unterwegs

The streetlights light up the corners. The rucksack is heavy. Granny's village is always really quiet after nine in the evening. Stefan turns round again. He thinks he sees a flame. And there's a very strong smell of smoke.

Ecken

Flamme

Rauch

Stefan starts to walk in the direction of the smell. Suddenly he sees a man running down the street. The man sees Stefan too. He is tall and thin, and has very short hair.

Richtung
Plötzlich

The man looks very worried when he sees Stefan. Then he runs away.

beunruhigt

"I must call the fire brigade," Stefan thinks.

Feuerwehr

He runs back to the phone box in the marketplace. Then he looks in his pocket for coins to make an emergency phone call.

Notruf

He finds the coins in his pocket. His mother put them there for emergencies. Stefan's hand shakes as he puts them in the telephone. He drops one coin and has to put it back in.

Then he dials 110. It's lucky that the phone box is there.

put – steckte ... ein

emergencies – Notfälle

drops – lässt fallen

"Hello, police station," a man's voice says.

"This is Stefan. There's a fire – in the marketplace!"

"Do you know the name of the street?" the man asks.

"No," Stefan says. "But I saw someone running away, too!"

"We're on our way," the man says.

Stefan replaces the receiver. He waits inside the phone box.

Then he realizes that he must phone his Granny. The smell of fire is worse now.

Has he got enough money for another call? Yes.

He dials her number. His Granny answers.

"I'm in the marketplace," Stefan says. "There's a fire near here. I called the fire brigade."

A fire engine arrives with a loud siren.

"Well, come home soon," his Granny says.

"All right. I have to go now. Bye," Stefan says.

Now Stefan hears more sirens. Two fire engines and a police car come into the marketplace.

legt den Hörer wieder auf

Großmutter

schlimmer

rief

Feuerwehrauto

Sirene

Stefan walks over to the policeman.

"I phoned you," he says, proudly.

"Thanks!" the policeman says. "You're out very late."

Stefan explains everything. The firemen pull out the fire engine ladder, and attach the water-hoses.

Then they start to put out the fire.

People run out of their houses to watch the firemen.

The fire is on the top floor of a house, and also in the cellar.

"That's strange," the policeman says.

He asks Stefan to describe the man who ran away.

rief an
stolz
erklärt
Leiter; befestigen
Wasserschläuche
Keller
seltsam
rannte

Stefan tells the policeman about the man.

Newspaper reporters arrive, and they ask Stefan questions, too.

The fire is now under control.

Reporter

"Just in time," the chief fireman says, and pats Stefan on the shoulder. "It's lucky you made that telephone call."

Gerade noch rechtzeitig

klopft

Everyone asks Stefan about what happened. He is proud. Then his Granny arrives and takes him home.

Großmutter

Two days later Stefan's Granny calls him downstairs.

"Just look at this, Stefan!"

His Granny points at an article in the newspaper.

"Wow! That's exciting!" Stefan says. And they both read:

Fire-Raiser Arrested
Ten-Year-Old Boy Helps Police Catch Criminal

Brandstifter; verhaftet

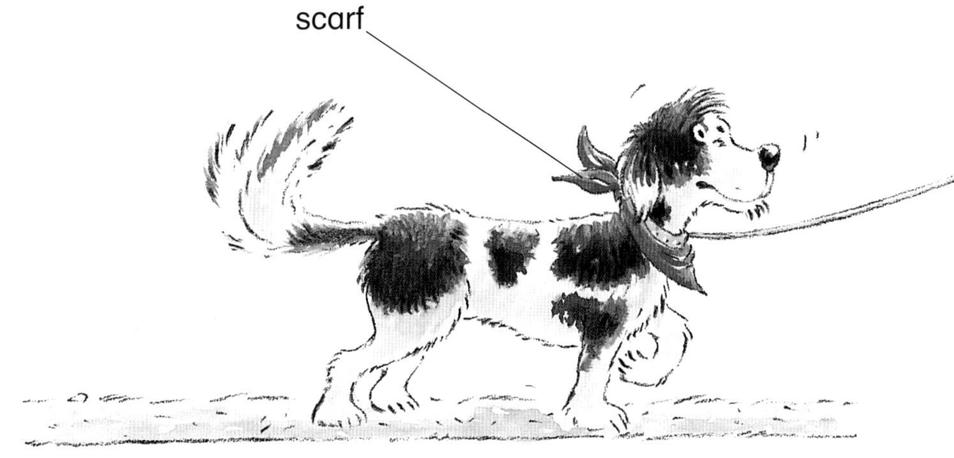

Trixi is kidnapped

Eva has a little brown-and-white dog called Trixi. She has a red scarf.

Eva is in a gang of five girls. They are in the same school as a gang of five boys. The girls think that the boys are stupid. One of the boys is called Leon, and he always has to look after his little brother Moritz.

One day, Moritz runs after his brother but then he gets lost.

Halstuch (scarf)
Bande (gang)
verirrt sich (gets lost)

The girls find little Moritz and wonder what to do with him. They don't want to take him back to his brother Leon yet because they don't like Leon. All the boys in Leon's gang are really stupid.

fragen sich · *Bande*

The girls lock little Moritz inside their special hiding-place – a garden-house belonging to Eva's aunt. Then they decide what to do with him.

sperren ein · *Versteck* · *das … gehört* · *entscheiden … sich*

Inside the garden house they can hear the sound of the little boy crying.

dem kleinen weinenden Jungen

"That's unfair of you," Lotte says. "Listen. I can hear him crying in there."

"Little children like him always cry."

wie

"Perhaps he's frightened. I think it's wrong to take away little children like this."

hat er Angst

"Don't you worry, Lotte, we'll take him back soon," Eva says.

"Well, I hope so," Lotte says. "He's younger than we are, and I don't think he likes being locked inside a garden house."

eingesperrt zu sein in

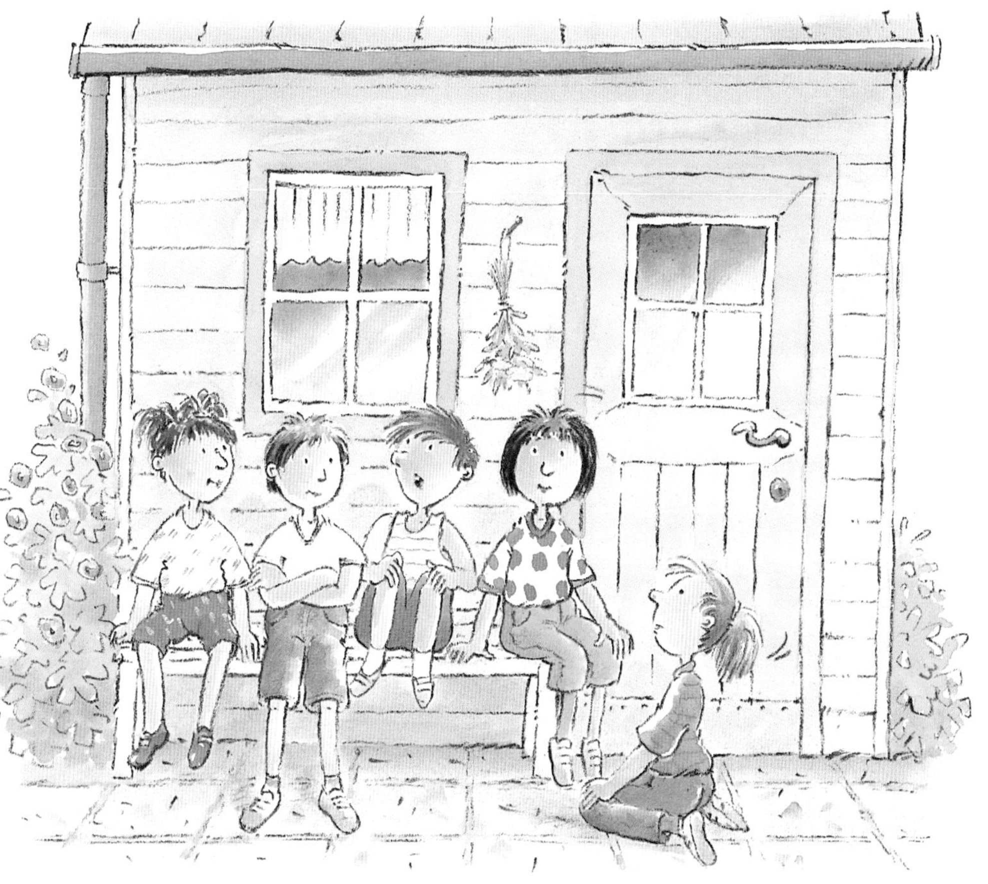

Suddenly the girls hear the special whistle of the boys' gang – and they run away. With the key to the house in their pockets!

Three hours later, the boys go away. Then the girls go back to the garden house.

They open the door quickly. Moritz is there on the floor, in the same place. He is very frightened and sad.

Plötzlich

Pfiff

Bande

hat Angst

"We'll take you home now," the girls say.

They take him back. Leon is in trouble with his parents because he lost his little brother.

The girls are embarrassed. They didn't want to steal little Moritz like that, and they didn't want Leon to get into trouble.

hat Schwierigkeiten

verlor

verlegen

The next day, Eva's dog Trixi disappears.

Eva looks everywhere: the cellar, the bedroom and the kitchen. No dog anywhere.

"I don't believe it! They've taken my Trixi!" Eva starts to cry. She can't believe it.

"What a horrible thing to do," Assy says. "But I think we did a horrible thing, too, when we locked up Moritz."

verschwindet

Keller

glaube

was für eine schreckliche Tat

einsperrten

She's right. They all nod. Then old Mrs. Schober says to Eva: "The boys came to get Trixi just now. They took the dog away."

nicken

Lotte, Assy, Luisa, Anne and Eva look everywhere. The only possible place is the shed. They go there.

möglicher Ort; Schuppen

"Eva, can you recognize Trixi when she growls?" Lotte asks.

(wieder)erkennen; knurrt

"Of course," Eva answers.

Eva goes over to the shed and tells the others to be quiet.

Suddenly she hears a whine. It's Trixi! But why can't she bark? Eva looks through the window into the shed.

Plötzlich; Wimmern; bellen

Trixi is there, with her scarf tied round her muzzle! What a horrible thing to do to a poor dog!

Halstuch, das um ihr Maul gebunden ist

Eva wants to rush inside the shed right away.

"Wait, Eva," Lotte whispers. She walks over to the boys. They are near the shed.

Lotte goes up to the boys and raises her hands.

"Peace negotiations," she says.

stürmen in

Schuppen

hebt

Friedens-verhandlungen

Eva is astonished. What is Lotte doing? The other girls are angry and confused.

"Peace negotiations," Lotte says to the boys. "What we did to Moritz was unfair. We want to apologize."

erstaunt

Friedens-verhandlungen

uns entschuldigen

The girls think that Lotte is right.

Lukas whistles at the other boys. They are all amazed by Lotte. — *erstaunt*

The boys go back behind the shed to discuss the situation. — *Schuppen; die Lage zu erörtern*

Finally the boys accept. But on one condition: from now on, they say, everyone must always try to be fair.

Lotte and the girls agree.

Lukas shakes hands with Lotte, and then with all the other girls. Everyone accepts the peace agreement.

Trixi is back with Eva. But something has changed now.

The five girls and the boys have joined their forces.

A gang of ten is far more interesting!

"And we're stronger, too!" says Lotte.

Trixi looks very happy.

She has her red scarf around her neck again.

Schließlich; nehmen an

Bedingung

von nun an

sind einverstanden

Friedensabkommen

hat sich verändert

haben ihre Kräfte vereint

Bande; weitaus interessanter

The stolen bicycle

"I want to try out my nice new bike, Mummy," Jakob says to his mother.

"All right, but be back in half an hour because we have to buy your new running shoes!"

"Okay, Mummy," Jakob says. He grabs his bicycle and cycles off.

grabs: schnappt sich

In the hall he hears something, but ignores it.

hall: Hauseingang

ignores: beachtet … nicht

"There he is." That is all Jakob hears. Then he cycles away.

Jakob turns down a forest track on his new bike. He pedals as fast as he can. The trees race past, and his speedometer says 40 kilometres an hour! He points his new helmet down further, and pedals as hard as he can.

Suddenly a man appears in front of him on the track. A big man with a moustache.

Jakob is forced to brake very hard. Two other men suddenly appear beside the first man.

"We've got you now, laddie."

"There must be some mistake," Jakob says.

He stands beside his bike. Then the men suddenly grab him.

"What do you think you're doing?" Jakob asks.

biegt ein
Weg
tritt in die Pedale
rasen vorüber
Tachometer
richtet
Helm; nach unten
weiter
Plötzlich; taucht auf
Schnurrbart
ist gezwungen zu bremsen
Junge

He tries to break free. But they say something very strange: “Aha. First he steals a bike and then he acts innocent.”

Jakob is frightened. But he can't shout for help, because

sich loszureißen

seltsames; stiehlt

tut (so); unschuldig

hat Angst

in the forest, no one can hear him.

"But I got the bike for my birthday last week," he says.

"Anyone can say that, laddie," they laugh. Then they grab his arm. "You come with us."

"But I didn't steal it, really!

"Shut up!" They grab his bike, and Jakob has to go with them.

"Come on, come on!" they say.

Then the men take Jakob to a bicycle shop.

Jakob is amazed. It's the shop where his parents bought the bike!

"We've caught him," the men say to the bike shop man. Jakob looks at the man and tries to say something. "Shut up," the men say.

Junge

habe … nicht gestohlen

erstaunt

kauften

Wir haben … geschnappt

"So, how did you manage that, laddie?" the bike shop man asks.

"Easy. The bike was here outside the shop," the men say.

The bike shop man doesn't know Jakob. His parents bought the bike one week earlier as a surprise birthday present for him.

wie hast du das geschafft

kauften

Überraschung

"But I'm not a thief! We can phone my mother, she still has the receipt for this bike."

The men continue talking.

The bike shop man starts to get suspicious.

Finally.

Quittung

reden weiter

misstrauisch

Endlich

"Should we go to your mother?" he asks.

"He's a liar," one of the men says. "Trying to get out of it!"

Sollen

Lügner

Er versucht sich rauszureden

They all talk again.

The bike shop man goes to the phone. He is clever. He quickly calls the police first, then he calls Jakob's mother.

He tells her: "Your son is here. He has a bike that was stolen from here. Some men saw him and they say he is the thief."

"That's impossible," the mother says. "We bought our bike. I have the receipt. Stay there. Perhaps," she adds, "the men stole the bike themselves."

The bike shop man puts down the receiver, and looks at the men. They want to leave. He winks at Jakob. Then he grabs Jakob's arm and whispers very quietly: "Help me to keep them here a bit longer."

was stolen – wurde gestohlen
impossible – unmöglich
bought – kauften
receipt – Quittung
receiver – (Telefon)Hörer
winks at – zwinkert ... (mit den Augen) zu

But the men are suspicious, and all three suddenly start to leave.

Just then, a police car comes round the corner.

The men run off. The police catch one of them.

misstrauisch

plötzlich

laufen davon

"Well, well," the bike shop man says. "Those bicycle thieves pretended that somebody else stole the bike!" He apologizes to Jakob, and gives him a reward: a big, shiny bicycle bell!

"Wow, thanks!" Jakob says. "That's just what I need!"

"You deserve it after all you've been through, my friend!" the bike shop man says.

pretended: taten so, als ob
stole: stahl
apologizes to: entschuldigt sich bei
reward: Belohnung; *shiny:* glänzende
That's just what I need: Das ist genau das, was ich brauche
deserve: verdienst
you've been through: was du durchmachen musstest

The moon rocket

"What do you want for your birthday?" Jana's mother asks.

"A moon rocket, of course! I want to be an astronaut, Mummy!"

Mondrakete

Her mother frowns. What can she do? It's impossible to buy a moon rocket as a birthday present.

runzelt die Stirn

unmöglich

Today Mummy has some time. She goes into town and looks for a present for Jana. She looks and looks.

Finally she finds a bedcover with rockets on, and a story book about rockets. Then she finds a special rocket-making kit for a plastic rocket, but it's only 40 centimetres high. Mummy knows Jana will be sad, but she can't find a rocket.

Schließlich; Bettdecke

Raketenbausatz

She buys the book and the kit. The bedcover is too expensive, so she buys a white one and then draws a big silver rocket on it, and underneath it the words: "Jana's Rocket".

darunter

The birthday is a real disaster. Jana wants a rocket and she doesn't get it.

She is angry and sad.

She shuts herself in her room, slamming the door loudly.

Mummy and Granddad eat the birthday cake by themselves.

Katastrophe

und schlägt … zu

Großvater

In the evening Granddad goes up to see Jana.

"Where are you, Jana?"

She is under her bedcover. Jana is disappointed. Her eyes are wet with tears.

Granddad sits down on the bed beside her.

"Why are you so sad?" he asks.

"You know why," she answers.

Bettdecke

enttäuscht

feucht von Tränen

"Shall I tell you a story?"

"If you like," Jana says.

"It's a story about a little girl who wants a rocket for her birthday. Her mother goes from shop to shop and asks 'have you got a rocket?' – but the people all shake their heads and say 'No.'

Wenn du magst

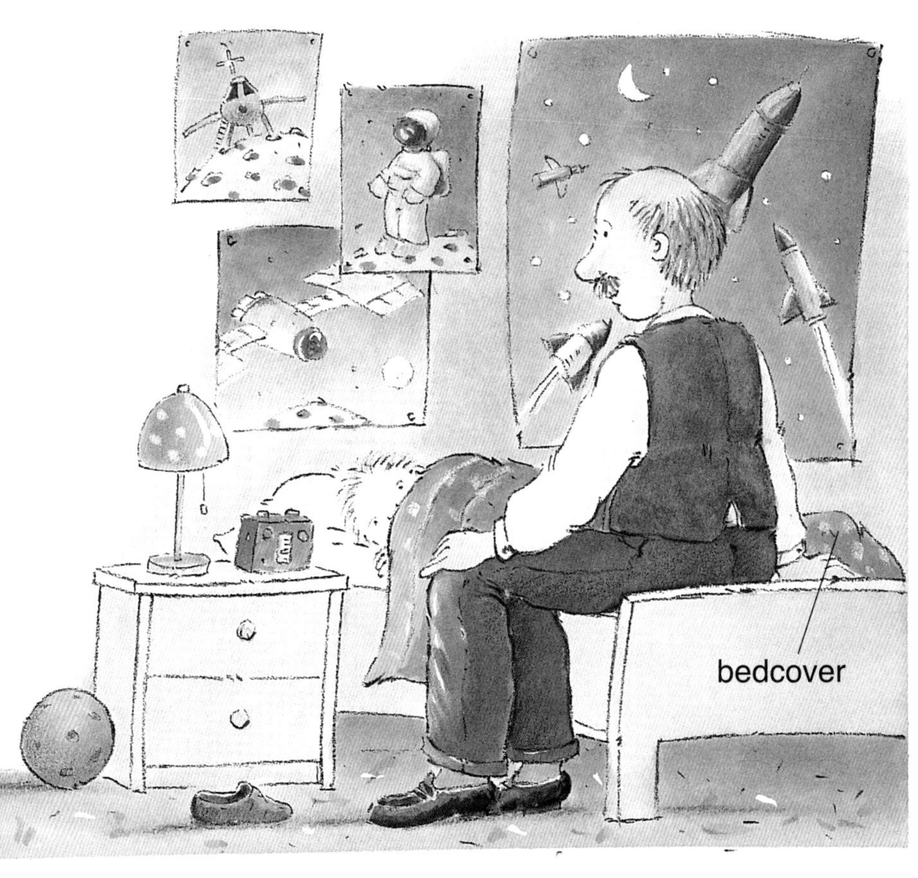

The mother goes home again. The father asks his friends: 'Does anyone know where I can get a rocket?' But they all shake their heads as well.

The grandfather writes a letter to an astronaut in America, but he is sad because nobody writes back."

Jana finally looks out from under the bedcover.

"Is that true?" she asks.

"Yes," her Granddad says. But the story's not over yet."

He takes a deep breath, and continues his story.

"The grandfather thinks of something very special. Since he can't get a rocket, he decides to visit an aircraft factory with his granddaughter. She wants to be an astronaut, so at the

Großvater

schließlich

Bettdecke

Geschichte ist noch nicht zu Ende

holt tief Luft

fährt fort mit

Da

beschließt; Flugzeugfabrik; Enkelin

factory she can see how aircraft are made. A big machine like an aircraft is very complicated. Astronauts have to know all about that. It's a very important part of their training."

"Is it really?" Jana asks.

Maschine
kompliziert
wichtiger

"Yes," Granddad says, and then he continues his story: "So the grandfather telephones the factory and makes an appointment for a guided tour – for Mummy, Daddy, Granddad and of course the little girl too."

"Is that really true?" Jana asks.

Her grandfather nods.

"And when does the tour start?"

"In half an hour," Granddad answers. "But we have to drive 20 kilometres."

"Well let's go!" Jana cries, and hurries downstairs to her parents.

Five minutes later they are all in the car. Jana is very excited. So are the others.

Großvater
fährt fort mit
Termin
Besichtigung
nickt
aufgeregt

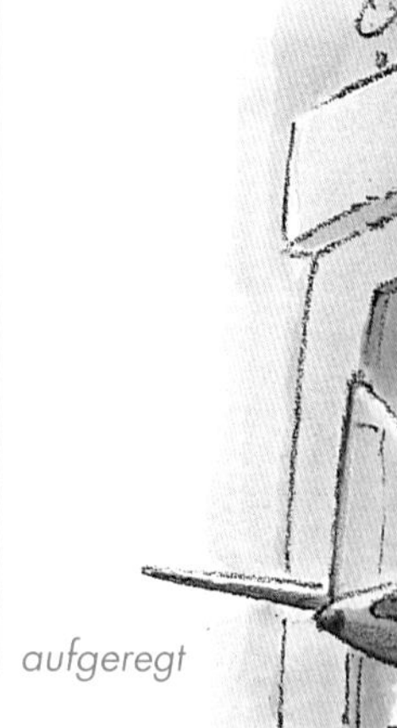

The traffic is not heavy, and they get to the aircraft factory quickly.

"Wow, look how big it is!" Jana says.

Es ist nicht viel Verkehr

Flugzeugfabrik

They go into the factory hall. Jana is allowed to sit in the cockpit.

"Planes are like rockets," she says. And starts to wonder.

Fabrikhalle
darf
Flugzeuge
überlegen

"Perhaps," she says, "perhaps I'll be a pilot."

"Or even an astronaut," her Granddad says.

Großvater

They all laugh.

She gives her parents and her grandfather a great big hug.

Umarmung

"You're the best parents in the whole world – and the best Granddad!" she tells them.

ganzen

"Even though we couldn't give you a rocket?"

Obwohl

"Yes. That was the best birthday of my life."

Then Jana says: "Some wishes just can't be fulfilled. And my rocket was one of them."

erfüllt werden

Shadows in the night

It's the start of the summer holidays. There is no rain tonight, and so Tina and Laura decide to sleep in a tent in the garden. They have airbeds and sleeping-bags from the cellar. It's very exciting.

Tina is almost asleep. She looks across at Laura – she is already asleep.

The garden is dark. The only light comes from the moon, and from a nearby street lamp.

decide – beschließen
tent – Zelt
airbeds; sleeping-bags – Luftmatratzen; Schlafsäcke
cellar – Keller
is asleep – schläft
street lamp – Straßenlaterne

Suddenly Tina wakes up. She looks across at Laura. The sleeping-bag is empty. Laura is not there! Tina is immediately wide awake. She looks round, and sees something moving. A shadow passes the tent! Is it a woman? Or a man? Where's Laura? The shadow starts to move faster now. Tina is terrified. Something has happened to Laura!

Plötzlich

Schlafsack

sofort hellwach

Schatten

geht vorbei (an); Zelt

hat fürchterliche Angst

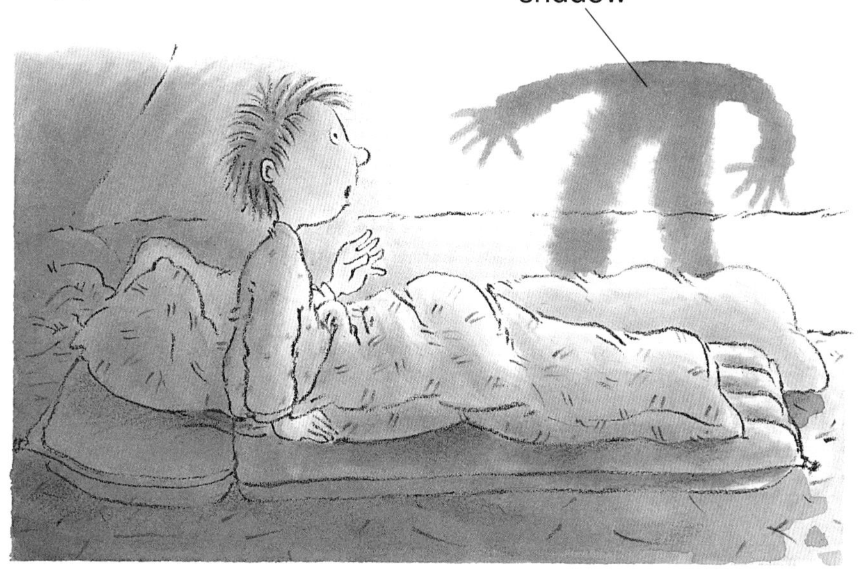

The shadow walks around the back of the tent now. Tina is so frightened that she can't breathe. Her heart beats very loudly. Help, Mummy! But Tina can't say a word. She shivers with fear.

Suddenly her nose starts to itch. She wants to sneeze. What did Mummy always say? Rub your nose.

Schatten
Zelt
hat … Angst
atmen; klopft
zittert vor Angst
Plötzlich
jucken; niesen
Reib

The itching gets better. She pinches her nose shut. Then it can't itch at all.

Jucken / *kneift*

The shadow comes closer again. Now Tina can't stop the sneeze any longer.

Schatten

"Atishoo!"

Total silence.

Völlige Stille

"They want to throw a sack over me," Tina thinks.

Then she hears Laura's voice! Laura pokes her head inside the tent.

steckt / *Zelt*

"Are you awake?"

Tina stares at Laura. What a question. And where are the men?

starrt

"I lost my necklace," Laura says. "On the lawn outside the tent. I didn't want to wake you up …"

Halskette / *Rasen*

"And I thought …" Then Tina tells her everything.

They sit together in the tent. Tina tells her about the shadows outside. And about her sneeze. The two girls take a deep breath.

"And did you find your necklace?" Tina asks.

"No." Laura is sad.

"What's this then?" Tina picks up something shiny from beside Laura's airbed. It's the necklace!

"Thank goodness," Laura sighs.

Laura snuggles back inside her sleeping-bag and says: "From now on, whoever wakes up has to wake the other person. Word of honour?"

"Word of honour."

Then the two girls go to sleep beneath the silvery moon.

Zelt
Schatten
Niesen
Halskette
Glänzendes
Gott sei Dank
seufzt
kuschelt sich
Schlafsack
wer auch (immer)
Ehrenwort
unter

Message in a bottle

Lissy and I play by the river sometimes. Mummy doesn't like it, but we really enjoy it. We like to skim flat stones across the water. Today the water is nice and flat.

Suddenly Lissy shouts: "Hey, look over there!"

I can see it too: "A message in a bottle!"

A green bottle, with a cork in it and a message inside, lying on its side in the water!

genießen
gleiten lassen; flache
Plötzlich
Flaschenpost
Korken
die … liegt

I quickly take off my shoes and wade into the water. Today the current is weak, so it's not dangerous. The river is very calm. I wade over to the bottle and reach for it – but suddenly it floats away from me. I get closer again, but each time it floats further away. It's a bit dangerous now, but suddenly I manage to grab it. A message in a bottle!

wade: wate
current; weak: Strömung; schwach
dangerous: gefährlich
calm: ruhig
suddenly; floats: plötzlich; schwimmt
manage: schaffe ich es
grab; message in a bottle: schnappen; Flaschenpost

I wade through the current with the bottle in my hand. My legs are covered with mud from the river bed. I hope I can get it off before Mummy sees it!

We both look at the bottle. "What if a genie comes out when I open it?" Lissy asks.

"Nonsense," I say to her. "Of course, it won't."

Lissy always thinks about things like that.

"But there might be one," Lissy says.

I start to wonder. Yes, there are genies and ghosts in bottles in fairytales … But surely not in real life?

wate; Strömung

mit Schlamm überzogen

Flussbett

bekomme es ab

und was ist, wenn …; Flaschengeist

Unsinn

wird nicht

Aber es kann einen geben

überlegen

Märchen

sicherlich

We decide to open the bottle. We sit down in the grass and hold the cork. It is wide at the top so we can hold it easily.

Lissy pulls at the cork, and I pull at the bottle. Then “plop!” – and the cork comes out.

No genie, luckily.

Instead, there is a big piece of paper inside the bottle.

We try to get it out, but we can’t. We shake the bottle, but the paper doesn’t fit through the narrow bottle-neck.

“We need a long pair of tweezers,” Lissy says.

“My Mummy’s got those!”

We take our bottle and run home as fast as we can. We run into the bathroom.

Mummy asks why we are so dirty. But I don’t even listen to her!

beschließen

Kork

zieht

Flaschengeist

engen Flaschenhals

Pinzette

After a lot of trying, we finally manage to get the paper out of the bottle. There is a message on it, saying:

schaffen es endlich

"Please write a letter, or visit us. Yours, William, Ghost of Sattemborough."

So perhaps it is a ghost after all! We turn the paper over and find an address on the back. We take out some writing paper and stamps and then write a letter to the address:

doch

Briefmarken

"Dear William, we have found your letter. Are you a ghost?"

haben gefunden

And one day a letter arrives! He writes: "I am a ghost, and yet I am not. I am a man, but only a little one." And he invites us to visit him.

und doch bin ich keiner

It takes a long time before we can persuade our parents to drive to Sattemborough with us.

dazu bringen

But then we go there. The rain is very heavy. We travel through dark countryside.

reisen

Landschaft

Suddenly we see a tower, and a wall – is it a castle? Or only a farm? We walk closer. We walk around the castle three times, and then the back door opens.

Plötzlich; Turm

A little man comes out and greets us: it is William. And almost immediately, a car arrives with his three grandchildren.

begrüßt

sofort

Enkeln

We stay with William in the castle for five days.

The evenings by the big fire are the best of all. That's when he tells us long stories about genies and ghosts and stormy nights.

Flaschengeister

Dein Wörterbuch A–P

A	after all	doch, eben, schließlich
	appointment	Termin
B	be fulfilled	erfüllt werden
	beneath	unter, unterhalb, (weiter) unten
C	calm	ruhig, still, friedlich
	complicated	kompliziert
	condition	Bedingung
	countryside	Landschaft
D	disappointed	enttäuscht
	down	her-, hinunter, nach unten
E	embarrassed	verlegen, in Verlegenheit
	even though	obwohl
F	finally	endlich, schließlich, endgültig

F	from now on	von nun an
	further	weiter, ferner, darüber hinaus
H	helmet	Helm
	hug	Umarmung
I	immediately	sofort
	important	wichtig
	impossible	unmöglich, ausgeschlossen
	innocent	unschuldig, ahnungslos
	inside	in
L	lawn	Rasen
P	past	beendet, vorüber, vergangen, ehemalig, früher
	perhaps	vielleicht
	place	Ort

Dein Wörterbuch P–T

P	possible	möglich, denkbar, geeignet
	proudly	stolz
S	since	seit, seitdem, vorher, zuvor, da
	surely	sicherlich
T	to accept	annehmen, anerkennen
	to act	spielen, sich verhalten, handeln
	to agree	einverstanden sein, einwilligen, übereinstimmen, vereinbaren
	to amaze	verblüffen, sehr überraschen
	to apologize	sich entschuldigen
	to be allowed	dürfen
	to be asleep	schlafen
	to be in trouble	in Schwierigkeiten sein
	to be late	zu spät kommen
	to believe	glauben, vertrauen, überzeugt sein, denken, halten für

T	to break free	sich losreißen
	to continue	fortfahren, fortsetzen, weitermachen mit
	to cross	überqueren, hinüberfahren, sich überschneiden, kreuzen
	to decide	(sich) entscheiden, sich entschließen
	to drop	fallen lassen, verlieren, (hin)-werfen, (herab-, herunter)fallen
	to enjoy	genießen
	to explain	erklären, erläutern, begründen, rechtfertigen
	to float	schwimmen
	to frown	die Stirn runzeln
	to greet	(be)grüßen, empfangen
	to ignore	nicht beachten
	to manage	es schaffen, zurechtkommen, verwalten, bewältigen

Dein Wörterbuch T–W

T	to miss	verpassen, verfehlen, versäumen, vermissen
	to nod	nicken
	to pass	vorbeigehen, -fahren an, weitergehen, -ziehen, -fahren
	to persuade	überreden, überzeugen
	to pinch	kneifen, zwicken
	to point	richten (auf), zeigen, hinweisen (auf)
	to poke	(an)stoßen, schubsen, knuffen, herausstehen, herumstöbern
	to pretend	so tun als ob, vorgeben, vortäuschen
	to pull	ziehen, zerren, reißen
	to race	rasen, jagen, rennen
	to raise	(auf-, hoch)heben, hochziehen
	to recognize	(wieder) erkennen
	to run off	davonlaufen, wegrennen